The Subtleties of the
Inimitable Mulla Nasrudin

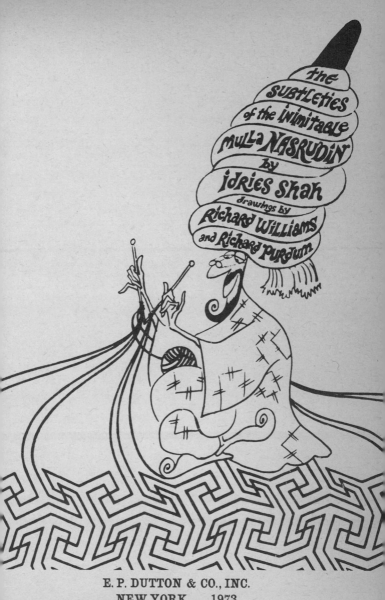

The Subtleties of the Inimitable Mulla Nasrudin

by Idries Shah

drawings by Richard Williams and Richard Purdum

E. P. DUTTON & CO., INC.
NEW YORK   1973

ISBN: 0-525-47354-8

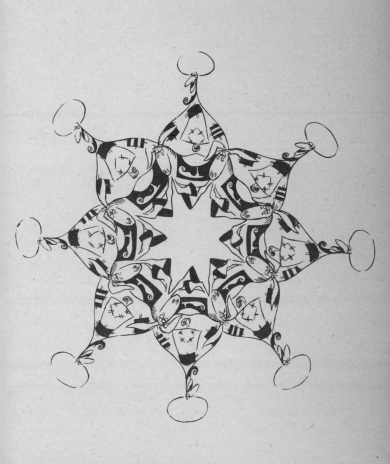

Acknowledgments

Many Nasrudin enthusiasts throughout the world have helped in the assembling of these tales. Their contribution has included translation, tape-recording, comparing variants, reciting stories, visiting immigrant communities and literary research.

We wish to thank all of them. Representatives are the following: Abdel-Karim Suhraverdi, Khan Abdul Karim Khan, Göte Evald Andersson, Sufi Anwar Ali Shah, Sardar M. Aqil Hussain Khan, *Barlas*, Don Ismael Benasar, Sir Edwin Chapman-Andrews, M. K. Chaudhury, Helena Edwards, Sheikh Fakhruddin al-Amudi, Sharif Faris el-Helebi, Feroz Abdali, Leon Flamholç, Hazrat Hafiz Abdullah, Bay Ilderim, Sayyid Iskandar, Jasim El Aneizi, Edward P. Lumsden, David Wade, Yar M. Khan and Dr Zeki el-Mahassini.

IDRIES SHAH
RICHARD WILLIAMS

Saying of Mulla Nasrudin

If I survive this life without dying, I'll be surprised.

Saying of Mulla Nasrudin

If I knew what two and two were – I would say Four!

Radio

When Mulla Nasrudin arrived at the immigration barrier in London, the officer in charge asked:

'Where are you from?'

Nasrudin said:

'Grrrr ... The East.'

'Name?'

'Mulla, ssssss, Nasrrrrgrrudin!'

'Have you an impediment in your speech?'

'Wheee-eee – no!'

'Then why do you talk like that?'

'Pip-pip-pip – I grr – learnt it from English By Radio!'

Where there's a will . . .

‘ ulla, Mulla, my son has written from the
Abode of Learning to say that he has com-
pletely finished his studies!’

‘Console yourself, madam, with the thought that God
will no doubt send him more.’

I might do you a favour

Nasrudin was penniless, but did not want his friend Aslam to know it. Unfortunately Aslam asked him for change for a gold coin.

'It is rather worn,' said Nasrudin.

'How worn, Mulla?'

'So worn that it is worth less than the rate of exchange. Try someone else.'

'No, I trust you. Give me just what you think it is worth.'

'Well,' said the Mulla, 'it seems to me to be worth so little that you would have to pay me something to take it off your hands.'

Needs

As the Mulla emerged from the mosque after prayers, a beggar sitting in the street solicited alms. The following conversation ensued:

Mulla: 'Are you extravagant?'

Beggar: 'Yes, Mulla.'

Mulla: 'Do you like sitting around drinking coffee and smoking?'

Beggar: 'Yes.'

Mulla: 'I suppose you like to go to the baths every day?'

Beggar: 'Yes.'

Mulla: '... And maybe amuse yourself, even, by drinking with your friends?'

Beggar: 'Yes, I like all these things.'

'Tut, tut,' said the Mulla, and gave him a gold piece.

A few yards farther on, another beggar who had overheard this conversation begged for alms importunately.

Mulla: 'Are you extravagant?'

Beggar: 'No, Mulla.'

Mulla: 'Do you like sitting around drinking coffee and smoking?'

Beggar: 'No.'

Mulla: 'I suppose you like to go to the baths every day?'

Beggar: 'No.'

Mulla: '... And maybe amuse yourself, even, by drinking with your friends?'

Beggar: 'No, I want only to live meagrely and to pray.'

Whereupon the Mulla gave him a small copper coin.

'But why', wailed the beggar, 'do you give me, an

economical and pious man, a penny, when you give that
extravagant fellow a sovereign?'

'Ah,' replied the Mulla, 'his needs are greater than
yours.'

This tale is reproduced by courtesy of Sir Edwin Chapman-Andrews.

The end of the world

'When will the end of the world come, Mulla?'
'Which end of the world?'
'Well, how many are there?'
'Two, the Greater and the Lesser. If my wife dies, that is the Lesser End of the World. But if *I* die – that is the Greater End of the World.'

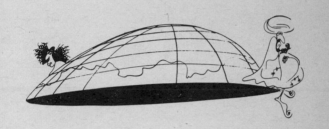

A bite

Nasrudin visited a stingy priest, who said to him:

'Would you like a bite to eat?'

When the food arrived, the Mulla saw that it was literally nothing more than a morsel.

At that moment a beggar looked through the window. The priest shouted:

'Go away, or I'll break your neck!'

'Brother,' said Nasrudin to the beggar, 'go away quickly, for I can testify that here, for once, is a man who isn't exaggerating!'

Gossip

'Mulla, your wife is a terrible gossip. She visits everyone in town and gossips all the time.'

'I don't believe that – otherwise she would surely have dropped in on me from time to time and gossiped – and she has never done that!'

Satisfied

 asrudin moved into a new house.

The postman called and said:

'I hope that you are satisfied with the mail deliveries.'

'More than satisfied,' said Nasrudin, 'and, in fact, from tomorrow you may double my order.'

Costly

asrudin opened a booth with a sign above it:

TWO QUESTIONS ON ANY SUBJECT
ANSWERED FOR £5.

A man who had two very urgent questions handed over his money, saying:

'Five pounds is rather expensive for two questions, isn't it?'

'Yes,' said Nasrudin, 'and the next question, please?'

Problems of loneliness

Something frightened Mulla Nasrudin as he was walking down a road. He threw himself into a ditch and then began to think that he had been frightened to death.

After a time he became very cold and hungry. He walked home and told his wife the sad news, and went back to his ditch.

His wife, sobbing bitterly, went to the neighbours for comfort. 'My husband is dead, lying in a ditch.'

'How do you know?'

'There was nobody to see him, so he had to come and tell me himself, poor dear.'

Arabic scholar

asrudin claimed that he had been to Mecca, and that he had lived a long time in Arabia.

'Tell us the name of a camel in Arabic,' one of his cronies asked in the teahouse.

'Why not have a sense of proportion,' said the Mulla, 'instead of thinking about such a huge creature?'

'What about the Arabic word for "ant", then?'

'Far too small.'

Someone called out:

'What is the Arabic word for "lamb", then?'

'I am sure they do have a word for them, but I wasn't there long enough to find out. I left just as the lambs had been born, and they had not the time for a naming ceremony.'

The problems of delay

The four-engined aircraft was in trouble, and the captain's voice came through the loudspeakers:

'One of our engines is faulty, but there is no danger. It will mean that we will be five minutes late, flying on only three engines.'

Some of the passengers were a little alarmed, but the Mulla, who was among them, spoke comfortingly:

'Five minutes does not make much difference, friends.' So everyone calmed down.

Soon afterwards, however, they heard the captain's voice again:

'Another engine is malfunctioning. We can manage on two engines, but it will mean that we will be half an hour late in arriving.'

Some of the passengers seemed uneasy, but the Mulla again addressed them:

'What is half an hour, after all? It is better than going on donkey-back!' The passengers accepted this philosophy, and settled down in their seats again.

Hardly another half hour had passed before they heard the pilot's voice again:

'I am sorry to have to inform you that a third engine is out of order. We shall be an hour late in arriving at our destination.'

Mulla Nasrudin said:

'Let's just hope the last engine does not break down, or we'll be up here all day!'

The forester

The forester was rather surprised to see such an unlikely figure as Nasrudin applying for a job.

'I'll give you a chance,' he said, 'although you don't look the type who could fell trees. Take this axe and chop down as many trees as you can from that plantation.'

After three days Nasrudin reported to him.

'How many trees have you felled?'

'All the trees in the plantation.'

The forester looked, and sure enough there were no trees left. Nasrudin had done as much work as would be expected from thirty men.

'But where did you learn to chop trees at that rate?'

'In the Sahara desert.'

'But there aren't any trees in the Sahara!'

'No, there aren't *now*,' said Nasrudin.

Moral: If you can fell trees, you can fell trees.

It takes one to know one

A practical joker challenged Nasrudin in the teahouse:

'People say you are very clever. But I bet you a hundred gold pieces you can't fool me!'

'I can, just wait for me,' said Nasrudin, and walked out.

Three hours later, the man was still waiting for Nasrudin and his trick. Finally he conceded that he had been fooled.

He went to the Mulla's house and put a bag of gold as his forfeit through the window.

Nasrudin was lying on his bed, planning his trick. He heard the chink of coins, found the bag and counted the gold.

'Good,' he said to his wife, 'kind destiny has sent me something to pay my bet with if I lose. Now all I have to do is to think out some stratagem to fool the joker who is, no doubt impatiently, awaiting me in the teahouse.'

Get the facts straight

 guide was taking a party round the British Museum. 'This sarcophagus is five thousand years old.'

A bearded figure with a turban stepped forward.

'You are mistaken,' said Nasrudin, 'for it is five thousand and three years old.'

Everyone was impressed, and the guide was not pleased. They passed into another room.

'This vase', said the guide, 'is two thousand five hundred years old.'

'Two thousand five hundred and three,' intoned Nasrudin.

'Now look here,' said the guide, 'how can you date things so precisely? I don't care if you do come from the East, people just don't know things like that.'

'Simple,' said Nasrudin. 'I was last here three years ago. That time you said the vase was two thousand five hundred years old.'

Moral: It's later than you think.

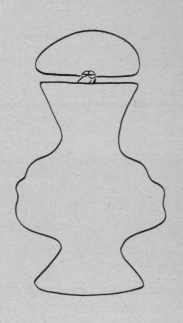

Cow with calf

The Mulla went to market to sell his cow, but nobody wanted to buy.

A neighbour came along and said:

'Let me try, you're doing it all wrong.'

'I must learn this art,' thought the Mulla.

'First-class cow, in calf for five months!' yelled the neighbour. In next to no time the animal was sold.

When he arrived home, Nasrudin found that a young man had called to inquire about marrying his daughter.

All the Mulla did was to try out his newly acquired skill. He was amazed by the speed at which the suitor rushed from the house.

Let's have it every day

asrudin strolled into a village in the middle of a feast. Food was pressed on him from all sides, there was singing and dancing in the streets, people took him into their homes and treated him like a king.

'If only our village was like this!' said the Mulla. 'Nobody gives anything away there … '

'But Mulla,' said the villagers, 'this is a special occasion, an annual feast-day … '

'Then I can make my own contribution in the field of ideas,' said Nasrudin. 'All you have to do (and we can do it in my village as well) is to institute annual feasts like this *every* day.'

The value of the man

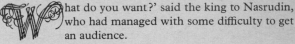hat do you want?' said the king to Nasrudin, who had managed with some difficulty to get an audience.

'A million gold pieces,' said the Mulla.

'Could you not make it less?' asked the surprised king.

'Oh, yes, I could make it – five pieces.'

'There is rather a disparity between the two sums, surely?'

'Yes. The million gold pieces is what *you* are worth; the five is what *I* am worth.'

Clearing the matter up

A dog had fouled the road between two houses. Each neighbour claimed that the other should clear it up.

Nasrudin was in court when the matter came before the summary judge.

This judge resented Nasrudin's claiming to be an adjudicator in common law. The case was difficult, so he decided to take Nasrudin down a peg or two.

'I will abide by your decision, Mulla Nasrudin,' he said, 'since this is a difficult case. You have the final word.'

'My decision', the Mulla immediately answered, 'is that since it is for the judiciary to clear up matters in dispute – *you* should clean it up.'

Hold that wolf

Nasrudin and a disciple went into a den to catch a wolf-cub.

Nasrudin went in first and found a fierce and full-grown wolf which attacked him. There was a terrible fight.

In the middle of the encounter, the disciple cried out:

'Stop kicking like that, I'm half covered with earth!'

'Yes,' gasped the Mulla, 'and if I stop what I'm doing, the other half of you will be covered as well.'

Miracles have details

ne day Nasrudin put a chicken to roast in his oven, and went out for a time.

A local wag substituted a live chicken.

When Nasrudin came back he found the house surrounded by villagers.

'Nasrudin,' they cried, 'Akram has performed a miracle. He has brought your roasting bird back to life.'

The Mulla opened the oven door, looked in, and then turned to face the crowd.

'Miracles are all very well, but there are certain matters of detail. Do you think that your power to work wonders, which I freely acknowledge on the evidence before me, gives you the right to theft? You have vanished my spices and salt. Who will pay for the firewood wasted? Worst of all, you have caused my effort in preparing the fowl to disappear.'

The water shortage

here was a serious water shortage in the Midlands. Due to lack of rain, the lakes which supplied a certain city's reservoirs were low.

The Council advertised for a water-diviner.

Nasrudin, who was working in a nearby factory, volunteered to help.

He stipulated that he would have to work at his water-producing on Monday.

When the day came, instead of taking a divining-rod, Mulla Nasrudin, surrounded by a crowd of curious spectators, took off his shirt, called for a tub and some water, and started to wash the shirt.

Every now and then he looked at the sky.

Someone protested:

'What has washing your shirt got to do with finding water for the city?'

'Patience,' said Nasrudin, 'for it is not the washing that does it. Every fool knows that it is just when you hang the clothes out to *dry* that the rain comes pelting down.'

Wife and secretary

'They have an interesting custom in England,' said Nasrudin, 'and it is one that I would like to copy.'

'What is that?'

'Businessmen take their secretaries to Paris and pretend that they are their wives.'

'But you haven't got a secretary!'

'I have thought of that. All I have to do is to take my wife to Paris and say that she is my secretary.'

How to keep it going

Mulla Nasrudin used to stand in the street on market-days, to be pointed out as an idiot.

No matter how often people offered him a large and a small coin, he always chose the smaller piece.

One day a kindly man said to him:

'Mulla, you should take the bigger coin. Then you will have more money and people will no longer be able to make a laughing-stock of you.'

'That might be true,' said Nasrudin, 'but if I always take the larger, people will stop offering me money to prove that I am more idiotic than they are. Then I would have no money at all.'

Cooking

ulla Nasrudin made nauseating meat-balls and sold them at a stall in the street, with a sign beside him inscribed: I REALLY WANT TO BE A STUDENT.

After a time the people of the town could not stand the sight or smell of Nasrudin and his meat-balls. So they made a collection.

'Go away and study, Nasrudin, for heaven's sake. Here is the money for it,' said their representative; 'and, by the way, what do you want to study?'

'Cookery!' said Mulla Nasrudin.

Must be one of them

There were twin brothers in Nasrudin's village, and one day he was told that one was dead.

Seeing one of them in the street, the Mulla rushed up to him:

'Which one of you was it that died?'

Mistaken identity

ulla Nasrudin was very ill, and everyone thought that he was going to die.

His wife dressed in mourning clothes and started to weep and wail.

Mulla Nasrudin alone was unperturbed.

'Mulla,' asked one of his disciples, 'how is it that you can face death with such calm, even laughing from time to time, while we who are not going to die are in torment lest you leave us?'

'Quite simple,' said Nasrudin. 'As I lie here looking at the lot of you, I say to myself, "They all look so terrible that I am almost sure the Angel of Death will mistake at least one of them for his prey when he comes visiting – and leave old Nasrudin here a while longer ... '

What's left

ulla Nasrudin went to a donkey market.

'Are you in the market for donkeys?' a merchant asked him.

'Yes,' said Nasrudin.

'What about one of these remarkably handsome beasts?'

'Just a minute,' said the Mulla, 'I want you to show me the *worst* donkeys you have.'

'Those are the worst.'

'Very well, then, I'll take the rest.'

The true and the false

The Mulla was thirsty as he walked on the seashore, and he stooped down to take a drink. The water tasted horrible, and he rushed to the village well, a good mile away.

'Quick, give me a pitcher of water!' he gasped out to a woman who was drawing some.

'Why, Mulla, are you thirsty?'

'Yes I am, but first I have to show an imposter what real water is like!'

First time

The Mulla was invited to a country house for the weekend.

His host had a number of horses paraded before the guests, so that each could choose one to ride.

The chief groom announced the horses:

'This one was ridden by Prince such-and-such; this one by the Duke of Blankshire . . .'

The Mulla was not to be outdone:

'Bring me', he said, 'a horse that has never been ridden at all.'

Tried to fool him

asrudin was at a football game. He had been shouting until half-time, and felt thirsty. 'I'm going to get a drink of water,' he told his friend.

'And one for me,' said the friend.

In a few minutes Nasrudin came back.

'I tried to have a drink of water for you, but I found, after I had had my own drink, that you were not thirsty after all.'

Moral: If you really want a drink of water, drink it yourself.

Diversion

Nasrudin went to see a football match. Twenty thousand spectators were milling around.

A man who was trying to buy a ticket from a tout turned to Nasrudin and said:

'I am going crazy! there are far too many people here.'

'You should have been here last week,' said Nasrudin.

'What, was it worse?'

'No, better. There wasn't a soul to be seen. No match that day.'

The marsh

One day Nasrudin was walking to town, when he saw some woods by the road.

'I wonder why people don't go that way, as a short-cut to the town,' he mused. He decided to try.

Halfway across, his foot went into a marsh, and his shoe came off, and was sucked under.

'All right,' he said to the mud, 'I know why now – give me back my shoe.'

The mud said nothing.

So the Mulla retraced his steps to the road, walked into town and then went back to the mud. 'Marsh, marsh', he said, 'I have given back the stolen time and effort to the short-cut: now give me back my slipper.'

No answer, so he reached into the mud and after a great struggle, he found his shoe.

'This mud is obviously determined to make everyone pay for his mistakes. But, although he is the keeper of the public conscience,' said the Mulla aloud, 'he is a hypocrite! Here is my shoe, right enough; but the mud has not only taken interest by making me struggle so much, he has dirtied the shoe as well.'

How to get out of trouble

A man had fallen between the rails in an Underground station when Nasrudin came along one afternoon. People were crowding around, all trying to get him out before a train ran him over.

They were shouting, 'Give me your hand!' But the man would not reach up.

The Mulla elbowed his way through the crowd and leant over to the man. 'Friend,' he said, 'what is your profession?'

'I am an income-tax inspector,' gasped the man.

'In that case,' said Nasrudin, '*take* my hand!' The man immediately grasped the Mulla's hand and was hauled to safety.

Nasrudin turned to the open-mouthed audience. 'Never ask a tax man to *give* you anything, you fools,' he said, and walked away.

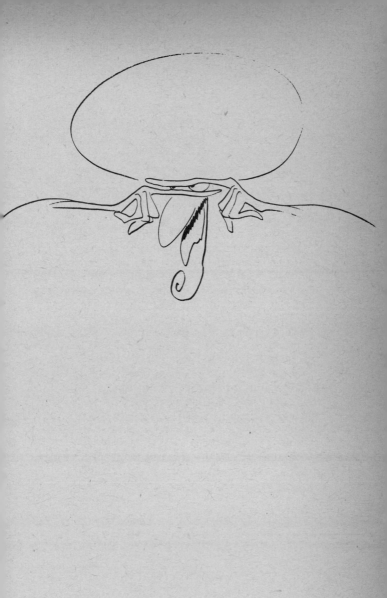

What could become what

akim went to a restaurant and ordered boiled eggs.

The crafty proprietor gave him a bill for five silver pieces.

Hakim protested that this was far too much.

'If I had kept those eggs and the hen had hatched them, they would have become chickens,' said the restaurant man, 'and their progeny, and theirs, and theirs, would have produced millions of eggs – worth much more than five coins. You have had your eggs cheap.'

The local judge was Nasrudin, and Hakim took his complaint to him. The restaurant man had to go along too, to defend his case.

Nasrudin at that time heard his cases at home, because he said that 'justice always appears in life.'

When he had heard the two arguments, Nasrudin took some corn and boiled it. Then he let it cool a little, and planted it, spoonful by spoonful, in his garden.

'Whatever are you doing?' asked the two.

'Planting corn, so that it will multiply,' said Nasrudin.

'Since when could something which had been boiled multiply like that?' burst out the restaurant owner.

'That is the judgment of this court,' said Nasrudin. 'Good day to you both.'

Large and small

Before Mulla Nasrudin became a Sufi, he used to think just like other people.

He went to pray for something he very much wanted in the Great Mosque. But there was no result, even though he went there every day for months.

When he confided his needs to another man, the other said:

'Why do you not try praying in the *takkia* of Sheikh Ahan? It is an oratory, like a small mosque, attached to the Sufi's house.'

The Mulla went there and tried again.

The very next day his prayer was answered.

Nasrudin went to the Great Mosque. Standing outside he addressed it with these words:

'For shame! To think that a baby mosquelet called a *takkia* could do what a grown-up like you cannot!'

Watch out!

'I wonder what I can do?' Nasrudin asked his friend Wali. 'People think I'm rude when I push my barrow behind them shouting "Mind your backs!"'

'No real difficulty about that,' said Wali. 'The English are cultured, and they don't like roughness, that's all.'

The two met again a few weeks later. Wali said:

'How are you getting on with your barrow?'

'Your advice was no good. I tried a bit of culture, but people still think I'm uncultivated.'

'What form did your cultivated behaviour take?'

'Instead of shouting "Mind your backs!", I yelled, at the top of my voice so that they'd be sure to hear: "SHAKESPEARE!" They got quite annoyed.'

They don't work

An engineer was fixing a bell outside a house. Mulla Nasrudin came by, stopped and asked:
'What is that thing?'
'Fire alarm'.
'I've seen them before – they don't work,' said the Mulla.
'What do you mean?'
'The bell rings all right, but the fire burns just the same.'

Stop-Go

ne evening Nasrudin was stopped by a policeman.
'This is a summons for driving through a "Stop" light.'

The Mulla said:

'When I go into court, I shall ask for it to be balanced against all the times I have stopped at the "Go" light and never been credited for it.'

Temperatures

Nasrudin was practising as a doctor.

A friend telephoned in the middle of the night.

'Come at once, I have a fever.'

'What's your temperature?'

'It must be 150 degrees!'

'You don't need me,' said the Mulla, 'you need a fire brigade.'

Time

asrudin was arguing with a man who knew far more about everything than he did. And, it seemed, he could also match every one of the Mulla's accomplishments.

Finally the challenger said:

'Nasrudin. Let us have a contest to decide who is better at everything. You propose something. No matter what it is, I'll guarantee to do it in half the time.'

'Accepted!' said Nasrudin. 'And until it is decided by these witnesses here, we'll be considered evenly matched. Here is my choice: we'll see after a thousand years of my lifetime whether you have aged only five hundred years.'

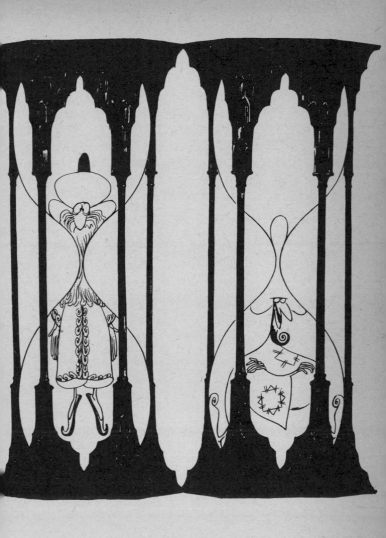

Feedback

asrudin was not feeling very well. He called in a doctor.

'You need a purgative,' said the physician.

'I want a second opinion,' said Nasrudin.

'An operation,' said the second doctor.

'Send for another doctor,' said the Mulla.

'Massage is the only answer in cases like this,' said the third leech.

'Now we have the prescription,' said the Mulla. 'A third of a cut, a third of a purge, and add one-third of a massage. That should clear things up nicely.'

Psychology

ulla Nasrudin went to see a psychiatrist. He said:

'My trouble is that I can't remember anything.'

'When did this start?' asked the doctor.

'When did *what* start?' said Nasrudin.

When to do what

ulla Nasrudin once disappeared from his desk for three weeks.

When he came back he was called into his employer's office.

'Where have you been, Nasrudin? You can't vanish for weeks on end without permission.'

'I was only following your instructions.'

'Explain yourself.'

'I went into your office to ask for a holiday. You weren't there, but I saw the notice on your desk – "DO IT NOW" – and so I did.'

The speed-traveller

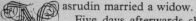asrudin married a widow.

Five days afterwards she gave birth to a son.

The Mulla went out at once and started to buy school equipment.

People asked:

'Why are you buying all these things?'

Nasrudin said:

'If my boy has accomplished a nine-month journey in five days, he will be ready for school any day now.'

It depends how you look at it

Trotting along on his donkey, Mulla Nasrudin was trying to eat some mulberry-flour. But each time he tried to empty some out of the bag into his mouth, the wind blew it away.

A passing farmer called out:

'What are you doing, Mulla?'

'At this rate,' said Nasrudin, 'I am not doing anything at all.'

Warning

Nasrudin entered the Land of Fools.

'O people,' he cried, 'sin and evil are hateful!'

He did the same thing every day for some weeks.

One day as he was about to start his lecture, he saw a group of Foolslanders standing with folded arms.

'What are you doing?'

'We have just decided what to do about all this sin and evil you have been talking about all the time.'

'So you have decided to shun it?'

'No, we have decided to shun *you*.'

Don't jump to conclusions

lthough he was supposed to be a wise and holy man, Nasrudin was accused of being almost illiterate.

One day the ruler of his country decided to put this to the test.

'Write something for me, Nasrudin,' said he.

'I would willingly do so, but I have taken an oath never to write so much as a single letter again,' said Nasrudin.

'Well, write something in the way in which you used to write before you decided not to write, so that I can see what it was like.'

'I cannot do that, because every time you write something your writing changes slightly through practice. If I wrote now, it would be something written for now.'

'Then bring me an example of his writing, anyone who has one,' ordered the ruler.

Someone brought a terrible scrawl that the Mulla had once written to him.

'Is this your writing?' asked the monarch.

'No,' said Nasrudin. 'Not only does writing change with time, but you are now showing a piece of writing done by me to demonstrate to someone how he should *not* write.'

Smooth trees

Nasrudin came from a small town whose mosque could not afford a minaret.

When he saw his first minaret, the *muezzin* was walking around the small platform near the top, calling the faithful to prayer at the four points of the compass.

Nasrudin called up:

'Before you got trapped in that peculiar position, you should have made sure that the tree was not so smooth that you could not climb down.'

Two for one

'Why are you dragging your wife towards the market-place like that, Mulla?'

'I have just had a brilliant idea. She is forty years old today, and I propose to exchange her for two twenty-year-olds.'

Myself

A monk said to Nasrudin:

'I am so detached that I never think of myself, only of others.'

Nasrudin answered:

'I am so objective that I can look at myself as if I *were* another person; so I can afford to think of myself.'

One man's meat

asrudin came home from a carnival in a terrible state, his Arab fancy-dress ripped to ribbons.

'Mulla,' said a friend who was waiting for him, 'you look as if you have been beaten up!'

'I have, indeed.'

'But people don't beat others up for wearing fancy-dress!'

'How can you explain that to Kurds whom you meet on the road, looking for Arabs to beat up?'

Salute

asrudin was passing through the Land of Fools one day, on donkey-back. On the road he passed two local worthies, plodding along on foot. 'Good morning,' said the Mulla.

'I wonder why he spoke to me, and not to you?' one of the fools said to the other.

'You idiot, it's *me* that he spoke to – not you!'

Soon they were scuffling on the ground. But then it struck them both at once that they could run after Nasrudin and ask him to settle the question. They jumped up and scampered after him.

When they finally caught him up, they shouted together:

'Which of us were you saying "Good morning" to?'

The Mulla said:

'The greater of the two fools!'

'That's definitely *me*!' said the first fool.

'Nonsense, it's obviously *me*!' said the other.

Nasrudin left them struggling in the dust.

The clock

'The Mulla's clock was always wrong.

'Can't you do something about that clock, Mulla?' someone asked him.

'What?'

'Well, it is never right. Anything would be an improvement on that.'

The Mulla hit it with a hammer. It stopped.

'You are right, you know,' he said, 'this really is an improvement.'

'I did not mean literally *anything*. How can it be better now than it was before?'

'Well, you see, before I stopped it it was never right. Now it is right twice a day, isn't it?'

Moral: It is better to be right sometimes than never to be right at all.

Not a good pupil

ne day Mulla Nasrudin found a tortoise. He tied it to his belt and continued his work in the fields.

The tortoise started to struggle. The Mulla held it up and asked:

'What's the matter, don't you want to learn how to plough?'

Ethological reflection

'Why, Mulla, don't you spend some time practising higher forms of thought, in order to improve yourself?'

'For the same reason that lions don't catch fish.'

'Oh, you mean that you are not equipped for it?'

'No, I only mean that I haven't got around to it yet.'

Quality and quantity

asrudin was taking a donkey-load of grapes to market.

Groups of small children kept begging grapes: but he only gave them a very small handful each.

'You are mean, Nasrudin!' they shouted.

'Not at all,' said the Mulla. 'I am doing this to illustrate the silliness of children. All these grapes taste the same. Once you have had some, you know what all the rest are like. So it doesn't matter whether you have many or just a few.'

Social conscience

omeone told Mulla Nasrudin that he should be as concerned about the welfare of others as he was about his own.

Accordingly, the next time he swallowed a mouthful of hot soup, he rushed out into the village street, crying:

'Beware, beware, my stomach is on fire!'

Bath song

The acoustics in Nasrudin's bathroom were un-usually flattering.

One day, captivated by the beauty of his voice, he thought:

'Why should I not share this delight with other True Believers?'

He rushed to the top of the nearest minaret and started to call the morning prayer.

Someone shouted up to him:

'Idiot! Not only is it not the time for prayer, but your voice is terrible!'

'Yes,' said Nasrudin sadly, 'we will have to wait until someone builds a bath up here before they will appreciate me.'

Wife, thief and donkey

The Mulla was tired of feeding his donkey. He asked his wife to do it, but she refused, and it all ended with a dispute in which they decided that whoever spoke first would feed the donkey.

The Mulla sat down stoically in a corner. His wife was soon bored and went to visit the neighbours. As supper-time approached she sent a boy with a bowl of soup for the Mulla.

In the meantime a thief broke into the silent Nasrudin household. He stole everything he could see. As the Mulla was sitting immobile and speechless, he even took the hat from his head. Then he left.

Shortly afterwards the boy with the soup arrived.

Nasrudin tried to explain with gestures that a thief had been there, but all the boy could see was that he kept pointing agitatedly at his head, from which the hat had been removed.

Taking the gesture as an order, the boy poured the soup on the Mulla's head and went back to report the strange circumstances to the Mulla's wife.

She hurried home. Seeing all the doors open and the cupboards empty, she started to curse Nasrudin.

Nasrudin said:

'Now go and feed the donkey, and look well at what you have achieved through your stubbornness.'

How much?

Nasrudin had saved a lot of money.

Someone asked him to go to a mannequin parade.

Afterwards he was asked how he liked it.

'It's a complete swindle!'

'Why?'

'They show you the women – and then try to sell you the clothes!'

The election meeting

t was before the elections. The town had invited all the candidates to address the citizens in the city hall.

Nasrudin was invited, as an exotic local character, to entertain.

When all three candidates had spoken, the Mulla mounted the platform and said:

'I have come here to offer you my own, special recipe. Make a note of this, and try it on yourselves.'

He went on to say that certain quantities of honey, garlic and fish were to be boiled together and then eaten.

Quite a number of people tried the recipe.

The taste was horrible. Several of them stormed Nasrudin's house, wanting to know what he meant by such a trick.

'Well,' said Mulla Nasrudin, 'I didn't say that I liked it, in fact I had not tried it on myself. But it seemed such a good idea to me, I wanted to see whether it would work. That's what election candidates do, isn't it?'

That's why they appreciate it

'Never give people anything they ask for until at least a day has passed!' said the Mulla.

'Why not, Nasrudin?'

'Experience shows that they only appreciate something when they have had the opportunity of doubting whether they will get it or not.'

A reason for everything

Nasrudin, starving with hunger went to a café and started to fill his mouth with food, using both hands.

His neighbour was passing, and stopped.

'Why eat with two hands, Mulla?'

'Because I haven't got three.'

What you hadn't thought of . . .

'If someone doesn't say something to entertain me,' shouted a tyrannical and effete king, 'I'll cut off the heads of everyone at court.'

Mulla Nasrudin immediately stepped forward.

'Majesty, don't cut off my head – I'll do something.'

'And what can you do?'

'I can – teach a donkey to read and write!'

The king said:

'You'd better do it, or I'll flay you alive!'

'I'll do it,' said Nasrudin, 'but it will take me ten years!'

'Very well,' said the king, 'you can have ten years.'

When the court was over for the day, the grandees crowded around Nasrudin.

'Mulla,' they said, 'can you really teach a donkey to read and write?'

'No,' said Nasrudin.

'Then,' said the wisest courtier, 'you have only brought a decade's tension and anxiety, for you will surely be done to death. Oh, what folly to prefer ten years' suffering and contemplation of death to a quick flash of the headsman's axe ... '

'You have overlooked just one thing,' said the Mulla. 'The King is seventy-five years old, and I am eighty. Long before the time is up, other elements will have entered the story ... '

Motive power

Nasrudin's little boy had been learning about books at school.

He came home one day and said:

'Father, could I have an encyclopedia to take to school?'

'No, you cannot.'

'But lots of the other children have got them.'

'I don't care about that. You just go on the train, like me and most other people.'

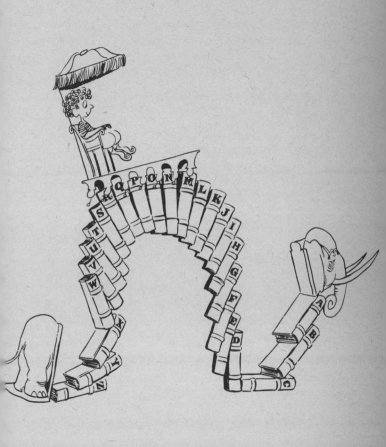

The right requirements

Someone asked the Mulla:

'Is it possible for a hundred-year-old man to have a child?'

'Yes,' he said, 'providing that he has an accomplice, say, in the twenties or thirties.'

Camel fodder

n Khanabad, Mulla Nasrudin was sitting in a teahouse when a stranger walked in and sat down beside him.

The newcomer said:

'Why is that man over there sobbing his heart out?'

'Because I have just arrived from his home town and told him that all his winter camel fodder was lost in a fire.'

'It is terrible to be a bearer of such tidings,' said the stranger.

'It is also interesting to be the man who will shortly tell him the good news,' said Nasrudin. 'You see, his camels have died of a plague, so he will not need the fodder after all.'

Tyranny of the majority

t one point in his life, the entire population of his village had had enough of the pleasantries and confusions of Mulla Nasrudin.

They all went to the magistrate, and he gave a ruling:

'Nasrudin, by the will of the people I have to declare that you must leave the village.'

'Are they unanimous?' asked the Mulla.

'Yes, I am afraid so.'

'Then I refuse to go. There are plenty of them – and only one of me. If they don't like the village as it is, they can leave and build another one. But I, a single individual, how can I even start to build one small house for myself elsewhere?'

A matter of language

Nasrudin went to a feast held by the Grand Lama of Tibet.

'You may not know our customs,' the interpreter told him, 'and so I must warn you that the Grand Lama regards it as very unlucky to sneeze.'

'I will remember that,' said Nasrudin.

All the grandees of the Lama's monastery were present, and in the middle of the feast, when a brazen horn was suddenly blown, Nasrudin sneezed right into the face of the Lama.

Afterwards the interpreter said to him:

'Our master is likely to have been most upset. Nobody has dared to sneeze here for a thousand years, out of respect.'

'Oh, I don't think you need to give it another thought,' said the Mulla. 'You see, I sneezed in my own language, not in his. He would never have realized what it really was.'

Too late

Mulla Nasrudin had been in England for several years. After settling in Liverpool, he had started to write poetry. He had composed thousands of verses and he and his friends had done everything they could to promote him.

His friend Wali found him sitting with his head in his hands, sobbing bitterly.

'Cheer up, Nasrudin,' he said, 'it can't be as bad as all that!'

'But it is,' said Nasrudin, 'for I have just discovered that I am no poet.'

All you have to do', said Wali, 'is to give up poetry – then you'll feel better.'

'But I can't do that. I've been elected Poet of the Century by the Academy of Culture. I've been famous since yesterday.'

Memory

'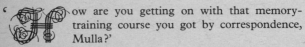ow are you getting on with that memory-training course you got by correspondence, Mulla?'

'I'm improving. Now I can sometimes remember that I have forgotten something.'

A hundred years

'What kind of birds should I stock my garden with, as a good investment?'

'Why, Mulla, I have just the thing for you – parrots, they live for a hundred years.'

'Well, you know how cautious I am. Just give me one to try out, and I'll be back if it does last the time you say.'

Nine donkeys

Nasrudin once undertook to take nine donkeys for delivery to a local farmer.

The man who entrusted them to him counted them, one by one, so that Nasrudin could be sure that there really were nine.

On the road his attention was distracted by something by the wayside.

Nasrudin, sitting astride one of the animals, counted them, again and again. He could make it only eight.

Panic-stricken, he jumped off, looked all over the place, and then counted them again.

There were nine.

Then he noticed a remarkable thing. When he was sitting on donkey-back, he could see only eight donkeys. When, however, he dismounted, there were nine in full view.

'This is the penalty', reflected the Mulla, 'for riding, when I should, no doubt, be walking behind the donkeys.'

'Did you have any difficulty getting them here?' asked the farmer when he arrived, dusty and dishevelled.

'Not after I learnt the trick of donkey-drivers – walk behind,' said Nasrudin. 'Before that, they were full of tricks.'

I only hope I'm ill

Nasrudin came late among the crowd waiting for the doctor's attentions.

He was repeating in a loud voice, over and over again:

'I hope I'm very ill, I hope I'm very ill!'

He so demoralized the other sufferers that they insisted on his going in to see the physician first.

'I only hope I'm very ill!' he shouted at the doctor.

'Why?'

'I'd hate to think that anyone who feels like me was really fit and well!'

The illness of my wife

'ood morning, Mulla,' said the local doctor, 'what can I do for you?'

'It is about the illness of my wife.'

'Is she ill?'

'Yes, she said that I'd better come to tell you that she would like to see you.'

'Shall I come at once?'

'No, she told me afterwards that she was feeling better, and so I've come to tell you that although you would have had to come if she hadn't got better, since she has recovered you don't need to come after all.'

Donkey lost

'Mulla, your donkey has disappeared.'

'Thank goodness I wasn't on it at the time, otherwise I would have disappeared too!'

Freakish

A man got into conversation with Nasrudin, standing outside a shop.

Nasrudin had a lot of stubble on his face. The man asked:

'How often do you shave?'

'Twenty or thirty times a day,' said the Mulla.

'You must be a freak!'

'No, I'm only a barber.'

The Company's time

he Mulla had taken a job in a factory. The foreman saw him lay down his tools and start to walk towards the door.

'What do you think you are doing?'

'I am going to have my hair cut.'

'You can't have your hair cut in the Company's time!'

'But I grew it in the Company's time.'

'Not all of it, you didn't.'

'All right, then, I won't have all of it off.'

Moral: You may have grown your hair in Company time, but this does not mean that everyone will understand you.

Grey and white

asrudin, when a child, asked his father:
'Why have you got grey hair?'
'Because, Nasrudin, children asking impossible questions make a man's hair white.'

'I see,' said the Mulla. 'That explains why your own father's hair is snow-coloured.'

Esoteric

A spiritual imposter named Khamsa once went to Nasrudin and said:
'Is it true that you have secret knowledge?'

'Tell me something of your own high experiences,' was all that Nasrudin would say.

'Very well. At night I leave this plane of materiality and rise to the highest heaven.'

'Do you, O Master,' inquired Nasrudin, 'feel that your face is being cooled by some fanlike object?'

'Yes, yes!' said Khamsa, thinking that this must be one of the indications of higher attainment.

'In that case,' said Nasrudin, 'you had better know that the fanlike object is the tail of my long-eared donkey.'

Automation

The management had called a mass-meeting of all employees.

'My friends,' said the managing director, 'I have to announce that, as from a month hence, this factory is to go over to total automation.'

There was a gasp from the whole audience.

'All processes will be carried out by machines. This will mean that the work is done better, more quickly and more profitably.'

'What about us?' someone called out.

'There is no cause for alarm. You will be paid as usual, with annual increments. You will continue to have the same subsidized canteen and sports facilities. All you will have to do is to come in on Fridays to collect your pay.'

Nasrudin, a union official, stood up.

'Not *every* Friday, I hope?'

Names

A certain conqueror said to Nasrudin:
'Mulla, all the great rulers of the past had honorific titles with the name of God in them: there was, for instance, God-Gifted, and God-Accepted, and so on. How about some such name for me?'

'God Forbid,' said Nasrudin.

The chalk

asrudin was chalking a slogan on a wall in London one day. Stopped by the police he acted in such a strange way that he was handed over to the health authorities, certified insane and sent to an asylum.

The asylum was full of dangerous lunatics. When he was pushed into the courtyard of the institution, the inmates crowded him with many a shout and scream.

He took his piece of chalk from his pocket. 'Stand back, everyone!' he shouted.

Surprised, the lunatics obeyed.

Nasrudin divided them into two teams, then drew a chalk line on the concrete between them.

'Now', he said, 'all of you jump under that. The first man under wins.'

There were terrible casualties as the teams dashed themselves again and again at the line.

Nasrudin was released. Nobody was quite sure whether it was because of the injuries of the inmates, or because of his resourcefulness with the chalk.

Moral: What got you into trouble may get you out again.

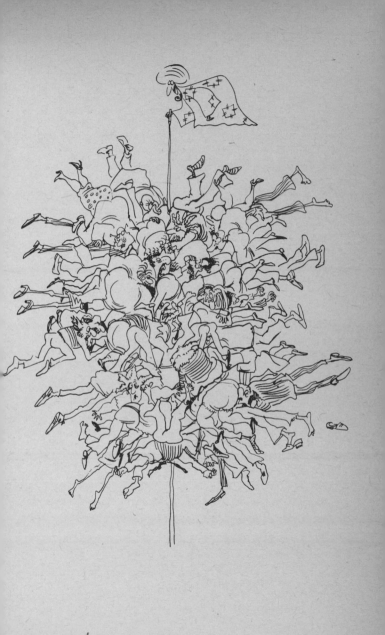

Lost property

ulla Nasrudin was walking through the streets at midnight.

The watchman asked:

'What are you doing out so late, Mulla?'

'My sleep has disappeared and I am looking for it.'

So hot

asrudin was very lazy. One day he returned from a trip to the Gulf, which is extremely hot in the summer.

'Do you know what?' he asked his fellow-villagers, 'I have never been so continuously active in my life as I was on the Gulf.'

'Whatever were you doing, Mulla?'

'Sweating.'

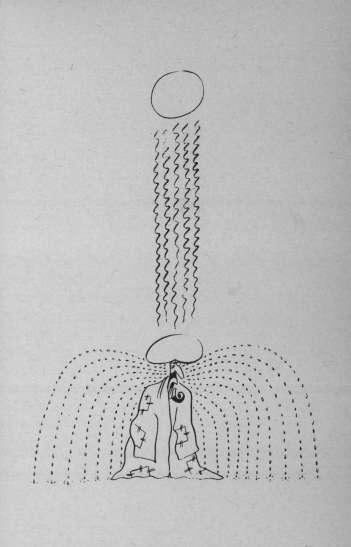

Is it me?

asrudin went into a bank with a cheque to cash.

'Can you identify yourself?' asked the clerk.

Nasrudin took out a mirror and peered into it.

'Yes, that's me all right,' he said.

Ambition

Nasrudin was being interviewed for employ-
ment in a department store.

The personnel manager said:

'We like ambitious men here. What sort of a job are you after?'

'All right,' said Nasrudin, 'I'll have *your* job.'

'Are you mad?'

'I may well be,' said the Mulla, 'but is that a necessary qualification?'

Moral: Ambition is all right, providing that you don't get in the other fellow's way.

Copyist

Nasrudin wanted to know more about art, so a friend took him to a gallery.

'Who painted that picture?' asked the Mulla, stopping in front of a huge and colourful canvas.

'Picasso – you can see by the signature.'

'The devil! How dare he copy my calendar?'

No relative

‘You are very ill, Mulla,’ said the neighbours. ‘Who are your relatives?’

'I haven't got any.'

'But surely you told us that your mother is alive?'

'She's alive all right, but since my father divorced her, I haven't a relative in the world.'

Service

Shoes

thief, who specialized in stealing shoes, followed Nasrudin one day.

The Mulla went into a mosque, sat down and started to say his prayers. Contrary to custom, he kept his shoes on.

The thief, who had sat down behind him, was unable to resist intoning audibly: 'A prayer said with the shoes on does not abide.'

'No,' muttered Nasrudin over his shoulder, 'but if the *shoes* abide, that is at least something.'

Two halves

asrudin opened a lecture agency. He knew so many people who felt that they had something interesting to say. Why not become their agent?

The ones who felt that they were interesting, however, were not usually interesting people. He got many complaints.

'Next time I shall make sure,' he said.

One day a telegram arrived from a study society: PLEASE SUPPLY A WIT TO ADDRESS OUR GROUP ON SUNDAY.

'This time I can make sure,' said the Mulla. He sent two of his lecturers, and replied by telegram: WITS DIFFICULT TO FIND SO HAVE SENT TWO HALF-WITS INSTEAD.

Moral: The sum of the parts is not necessarily equal to the whole.

Problem of communication

'Language', said Mulla Nasrudin, 'was devised to describe actions as well as thoughts. That means that all you have to do is to get the words right, and everything will be understood.'

'But Mulla,' said a friend, 'surely that cannot apply to everything?'

'Yes, it should.'

'Then can you describe to me how the silk industry is carried out?'

'Certainly. The first part is to get the worms and untwist that which is twisted. The second part is to get rid of the worms and retwist that which has been untwisted.'

The trip

asrudin's friend Wali slipped and fell from the immense height of the Post Office Tower in London.

The following night, Nasrudin dreamt that he was visiting Heaven when he ran across Wali.

'What was it like, Wali?'

'The impact was terrible, but the trip – the trip was terrific!'

The same strength

Nasrudin attended a lecture by a man who was teaching a philosophy handed down to him by someone who lived twenty years before.

The Mulla asked:

'Is this philosophy, in its present form, as applicable today, among a different community, as it was two decades ago?'

'Of course it is,' said the lecturer. 'That is just an example of the ridiculous questions which people ask. A teaching always remains the same: truth cannot alter!'

Some time later, Mulla Nasrudin approached the same man for a job as a gardener.

'You seem rather old,' said the lecturer, 'and I am not sure that you can manage the job.'

'I may look different,' said Nasrudin, 'but I have the same strength I had twenty years ago.'

He got the job on the strength of his assurance.

Soon afterwards, the philosopher asked Nasrudin to shift a paving-stone from one part of the garden to another. Tug as he might, the Mulla could not lift it.

'I thought you said that you were as strong as you were twenty years ago,' said the sage.

'I am,' answered Nasrudin, 'exactly as strong. Twenty years ago I could not have lifted it, either!'

Second thoughts

undreds of people were streaming away from the evening meeting of a certain Sufi, while Nasrudin was making his way towards the house.

Suddenly Nasrudin sat down in the middle of the road. One of the people stopped and asked:

'What are you doing?'

Nasrudin said:

'Well, I *was* going to the house of the Sufi. But since everyone else is going *away* from it, I'm having second thoughts.'

How to catch Nasrudin

f you want your donkey to move faster, Nasrudin', said a neighbour, 'get some ammonia and rub it on its rump.'

Nasrudin found that this worked.

One day, feeling a little listless, he tried the same remedy on himself.

The ammonia burned him so much that he started to run round and round his room.

'What's the matter?' shouted his wife, unable to get hold of him.

'If you want to catch me, use the contents of that bottle over there,' panted Mulla Nasrudin.

The will of Allah

' ay the will of Allah be done,' a pious man was saying about something or other.

'It always is, in any case,' said Mulla Nasrudin.

'How can you prove that, Mulla?'

'Quite simply. If it wasn't always being done, then surely at some time or another *my* will would be done, wouldn't it?'